CONTENTS

The water we drink and the air we breathe are essential to keep us alive. Coal, oil and gas provide energy to keep us warm, give us fuel for our cars and power for our industries. We burn fuels in power stations to make electricity, which means we can switch on lights and run our fridges and washing machines. Wood, brick and stone are other resources we rely on to build our homes. These are all materials that come from our environment.

New houses use up many natural resources.

ENERGY AND RESOURCES

FOOD AND GROWTH

Fertile soil, fresh air, sunshine and rain, plus water from the earth's rivers and lakes, are the natural resources that plants and trees use to grow. Farmers also rely on these resources to grow crops to provide food for animals and people. But crops are only good to eat if the air, rain and water are clean. If the air is full of smoke, or the water or soil is polluted, then the crops will be poor or may not grow at all.

A West African farmer shows crops of millet and sorghum grown in a year when the rains were good (left hand), and the same foods when the rains failed (right hand).

GROWTH AND DECAY

Plants have a natural order of new growth at the start of the year and decay at the end of the year. In the autumn, fruits are produced, leaves die and seeds are scattered; the next year new life begins again. For some plants this whole process takes only one year, but many trees grow very slowly. It can take many years for some trees to be replaced.

Autumn leaves fall, continuing the cycle of growth and decay.

HIDDEN TREASURE

Some natural resources, such as coal and oil, take millions of years to develop. They are the remains of old forests, buried when the earth was young. The trees rotted away, taking on the different forms of coal, oil and gas. Stored deep underground, they are called fossil fuels.

Coal is used to heat iron ore in a German blast furnace in order to extract the pure metal to make steel.

We have discovered where these deposits of fossil fuels lie and how to dig them up and use them. In a similar way, we dig up chalk and sand to make cement, iron ore to make steel, and silver to make jewellery. There is a constant search for more of these valuable underground treasures.

Until 100 years ago, large parts of the world were still unknown. There were always new places to explore and live. People were surrounded by seemingly plentiful supplies of wood for building, water for drinking and land to cultivate for food.

Rainforests still hold many mysteries.

LIMITED RESOURCES

In Nigeria, a Boram woman digs for water for her family in a dry river bed.

RUNNING OUT

As recently as the 1960s, people began to realize that there was a limit to the riches of our planet. The forests could not renew themselves as quickly as people could cut them down. In Africa and the Middle East, there was not enough water for the growing populations. Governments across the globe realized that coal, gas and oil could be running out too. They saw that many resources, once thought of as plentiful, might soon become scarce.

DAMAGE AND POLLUTION

Just as worrying as resources running out is the damage done to the environment by pollution. Car exhausts and smoke from factories make the air dirty. In places, rain no longer falls as clean water, but contains acid from the smoke, killing trees and damaging buildings. Sewage and chemicals drain into rivers and seas, harming fish and making animals and humans who drink the water sick.

Acid rain caused by pollution from factories has killed this once healthy forest in the former Czechoslovakia.

Waste from a chemicals factory in Mexico makes this water unusable.

BRUNDTLAND REPORT

In 1983, because of the concern about resources running out and the damage done by pollution, a World Commission on Environment and Development was set up by the United Nations. The then Prime Minister of Norway, Mrs Gro Harlem Brundtland, was in charge. She said the people of the world must change the way they lived. If they did not do so all the fertile land and forests would be used up. All the coal, oil and gas would run out. Future generations would have nothing left to live on.

Gro Harlem Brundtland warned that the earth's resources will run out.

In June 1992 all the world's leaders gathered at Rio de Janeiro, Brazil, at the biggest conference ever held. The United Nations Conference on Environment and Development, the 'Earth Summit', was to try and reach world agreement to limit the damage being done by people to the environment.

In 1997, Earth Summit II was held to check improvements to the environment.

RESOURCES AND AGENDA 21

Energy-saving technology, such as solar power, must be made available to developing countries.

A PLAN FOR THE FUTURE

All the leaders at the Summit signed an agreement called Agenda 21. This is a practical plan to enable people to live comfortable lives, while at the same time making sure that the children of the future do not suffer because people today have used up too many of the world's resources. This is called 'sustainable development'.

'The Chinese have a proverb: "If a man cheats the earth, the earth will cheat the man".'
United States President Bush at the Earth Summit.

This plan recognizes the need for countries to invest in industry in order to be able to offer their people a good standard of living. It also recognizes that to solve the world's problems, all nations must work together, sharing knowledge and technology. In this way, each country can develop, but cause as little pollution as possible.

Here are some of the most important aims of Agenda 21 for preserving the earth's resources:

- limit the amount of pollution in the atmosphere and stop the world's climate heating up too much
- protect fresh water supplies and share what is available
- prevent forests being destroyed and replant as many trees as possible
- prevent plants and animals becoming extinct by preserving their habitats
- preserve resources by re-using materials and developing alternative sources of energy from the sun, wind and waves
- stop the spread of deserts

9

CASE STUDY

THE RHINE

SAVING A RIVER

The river Rhine is the largest European river running into the North Sea. Twenty years ago it became so polluted that fish died and people living along the banks were no longer able to use the water for drinking. The countries which the river runs through – Switzerland, France, Germany and the Netherlands – got together and decided to clean up the water. The river is still not perfect but nearly all chemical and sewage discharges into the river have been stopped. The fish have returned and the water can once again be used for drinking.

The clean-up of the Rhine was one of the first successful international schemes to save a river.

AGENDA 21 aims to:

- clean up the air
- cut pollution
- slow global warming
- reduce the hole in the ozone layer

Less pollution, less illnesses like asthma.

THE AIR WE BREATHE

The earth is warmed by the sun. As sunlight passes through the atmosphere (the gases that surround the earth) it heats up the ground. The heat escapes back into space at night, but the speed it goes depends on the mixture of gases in the air. Air is made up of many gases, such as oxygen and carbon dioxide. If the amount of carbon dioxide is increased the heat from the ground escapes more slowly and, over time, the earth heats up. Scientists today are concerned that the world is heating up too fast.

Clouds made of water vapour and other gases stop sunshine reaching the earth, but also trap heat near the ground and prevent it from escaping.

A CHANGE IN AIR

When we burn fossil fuels and wood extra gases, including carbon dioxide, are released into the air via the smoke. These gases trap the earth's heat near its surface, acting like the glass in a greenhouse. Experts have called the resulting warming of the earth 'global warming', or the 'greenhouse effect'. Air pollution also affects people's health, causing asthma and other illnesses.

Black smoke from bonfires, factories and cars can cause a health risk and damage the environment.

A PROTECTIVE LAYER

High in the sky, there is a layer of gas called ozone which protects the earth from being burnt by the sun. This protective layer is being damaged by manmade chemicals which have escaped into the atmosphere from machines such as fridges. Holes are appearing in the ozone layer, allowing too much sunshine through which can cause skin cancers. Now everyone has realized the danger to the ozone layer, these chemicals are being banned.

Old fridges are dumped, but the chemicals used in them can be recycled to prevent harm to the ozone layer.

'Everyone should have the right to breathe clean air.'

AGENDA 21

CASE STUDY

UNITED STATES

LESS FUEL CREATES LESS POLLUTION

Designers at General Motors have built a four-passenger car without using steel, which makes the car lighter. The low weight of the car, combined with its slim sports car design, allows it to use the same amount of fuel as a normal car but to go nearly three times as far.

The need for less fuel not only means preserving resources, but also cuts the level of pollution.

AGENDA **21** aims to:

- provide clean water for all
- promote the sharing of water resources
- stop the waste and pollution of water

MANAGING WATER

WATER FOR SURVIVAL

Water is one of our most important resources – we cannot survive without it. Since the beginning of civilization people have built their homes next to rivers and used water for drinking and cooking. Water also provides power and transport. Yet the earth's waterways are under constant stress.

In most developed countries, all people have to do to get clean water is to turn on a tap. But even in these countries there is not enough water to meet people's needs.

In the last 50 years, schemes to dam rivers have increased: more and more water is taken out of the waterways to meet the needs of growing populations. For example, by the time the great Colorado River in the United States reaches the sea, it is reduced to a trickle. Much of its water has been taken out for the needs of giant cities such as Los Angeles.

(Top) Sprinkler systems to keep gardens beautiful in the summer are wasteful if other people need the water to drink.

(Above right) Bonneville Dam in the USA is just one of eight dams taking water from the Columbia-Snake River.

ACCESS TO WATER

In developing countries, such as Africa and India, access to water is not always straightforward. It is the custom for women in some communities to fetch water for their families. They often have to walk many miles to get enough water for cooking, drinking and washing. Children sometimes die of disease because the water is dirty and full of germs and viruses. The problem for their mothers is that there is no clean water to give them, but without any water at all the children will die of thirst.

In Africa, women often walk miles to collect water for their families.

CASE STUDY

AFRICA

A CLEAN SUPPLY OF WATER

In Africa and other countries where industry and technology is not very advanced people need help to find and use water properly. Organizations such as WaterAid teach people how to dig wells and provide simple pumps to draw up the water. Women and their children are taught not to use dirty water for drinking and waste water is kept away from the clean supplies. Simple, basic sanitation is installed at the same time.

A simple pump to tap underground water makes life much easier in developing countries.

Governments are sometimes forced to place bans on watering crops to save enough water for people to drink and wash.

'Many of the wars of this century were about oil, but wars of the next century will be about water.'

Ismail Seageldin, Vice President of the World Bank, 1995.

14

WATER SHORTAGES

Proper water management means that a country can benefit from its rain fall all year round. By holding back the winter rainfall, and stopping it from running into the sea, water shortages in the summer can be prevented. Additionally, water which has been used can be cleaned and used again to irrigate crops or top up the level of rivers.

Water needs to be managed and shared out carefully, otherwise situations can get out of hand. Problems arise when the people from one country take water that others downstream believe should have been left for their use.

The River Nile in Africa flows through eight countries, all of which need to use water from the river. Egypt, closest to the sea, has the largest army of these countries. Officials have threatened to attack all those higher up the river if they use more water and Egypt does not get its fair share.

Collecting water when it rains is an important exercise whether it is in a reservoir (above) or in simple pots and containers (left).

THE CLEANING-UP PROCESS

Now, all developed countries treat waste water. Water passes through to sewage works where waste and chemicals are removed. The clean water is then put back into the river to be used again.

Water from the River Lea, a river running off the Thames near London in the UK, is used seven times. It has travelled through seven taps, been drunk by seven lots of people, passed through seven sewage works, and been put back into the River Lea as clean water seven times before it flows into the River Thames and then out to the sea.

Thames Water Company check every day to see that the river water is clean.

CASE STUDY

NEW YORK CITY

CONSERVING RESOURCES

In New York, the water company decided to replace 1.3 million toilets and a million shower heads to save water. The old toilets used 18 litres of water for each flush; the new design uses only 6 litres. It cost the company $250 to replace each toilet, but it was quicker, cheaper and better for the environment than building the giant new reservoir that was otherwise needed. Demand for water has gone down in New York as a result of the changes.

The many customers in New York are very happy with their new toilets and showers, provided free of charge.

AGENDA 21 aims to:

- halt deforestation
- promote the planting of millions of new trees
- show how to use and value forest products
- encourage society to leave forest tribes in peace

Rainforests help control the climate.

CUTTING DOWN THE FORESTS

Trees are vital for many reasons. Wood from trees has been used by people over thousands of years to make life easier and more comfortable. Throughout history wood has been a main building material. It is also used to keep us warm and to provide heat for cooking.

'National action programmes to plant trees and allow damaged forests to regrow should be established.'

AGENDA 21

Although concrete and steel are now widely used, wood still forms part or all of many buildings throughout the world.

Trees provide food and shelter. Hundreds of trees together make a forest. When it rains on forests, water soaks into leaves, roots and fallen debris. The water leaks out gradually into streams and rivers. By holding back rainwater in this way, trees help to stop flooding. As water evaporates from forests, clouds form and create rain in other places.

LIVING AND BREATHING

Trees help to keep the air we breathe from becoming too polluted. Trees live by taking carbon dioxide from the air, using sunlight and taking food from the soil. Carbon dioxide is a gas, but trees turn it into a form of solid carbon in order to grow. Forests help prevent global warming by storing surplus carbon dioxide. While doing all this good work, trees also make oxygen and release it into the air. Humans and animals use oxygen to breathe and stay alive. In turn, they breathe out carbon dioxide.

Trees are so important there are many projects to protect and grow them. Here, women tend a tree nursery in Bangladesh.

17

CASE STUDY

SOUTH AMERICA

FARMING THE FOREST

In South America experts have worked out that keeping an acre of trees is more valuable than cutting the trees down and turning the land over to cattle for grazing. Fruit gathered in the forest can be sold, creepers can be used to make rope, sap from trees can be collected to make rubber for car tyres. All this means managing the forest carefully to produce several crops at once. It is called farming the forest and is an example of sustainable use.

As well as providing valuable products, trees prevent deserts forming by holding soil together with their roots.

DISAPPEARING FORESTS

Once most of the world's land surface was covered in trees. For thousands of years, however, people have been clearing trees to obtain wood for building and fuel, and to provide land to grow crops, or graze sheep and cattle.

'The traditional homes and lifestyles of forest dwelling peoples should be preserved.'

AGENDA 21

The destruction of the rainforest is happening at a great speed.

Yanomami tribal farmers of the Venezuelan Amazon live in harmony with their environment.

In the last 50 years forests have been cut down at an alarming rate. While the demand for wood has grown, farmers, too, have cleared forests in order to get more land. The homes of many plants and animals have disappeared and people from forest dwelling tribes have been driven from their villages.

Deforestation has also altered the climate – in places it no longer rains and farmers have lost their land to spreading deserts.

In Washington State, in the US, the destruction of the rainforest is plain to see.

18

A FUTURE AIM

Europe was once covered in forests, now four-fifths of the continent is covered in cities, farms, roads and barren land. All countries in Europe are now planting new trees. The United Kingdom, with only 5% of its land area covered in trees (the smallest percentage of any country in Europe) is aiming to double the number of trees by 2050.

Ninety-four per cent of the world's remaining forests is still unprotected from being cut down.

Once forests, much of the UK countryside is now farm land.

19

CASE STUDY

ACROSS THE GLOBE

MANAGING THE FORESTS

The World Wide Fund for Nature, together with other environmental groups, timber traders, foresters and shops, has begun the Forest Stewardship Council (FSC) to encourage good forest management worldwide. It awards a special FSC label to products made from wood that come from forests where the environment and the well-being of local people are being taken care of. Where products show the FSC logo, you can be confident that they come from well-managed forests.

The FSC label helps shoppers to identify items which have been made from wood from well-managed forests.

THE VARIETY OF LIFE

Every handful of earth and drop of water is full of life, often tiny specks that can only be seen through a microscope. Deep in forests or oceans and in the middle of deserts, there are large and small creatures alike, many yet to be discovered by people. The world is truly a wonderful place with millions of creatures, plants and trees that have each adapted to live and thrive in different conditions. This vast range of species is called bio-diversity.

All over the earth, there are different forms of life. Some plants or animals appear in many different habitats. Others may only appear in one specialized environment, such as on the desert floor.

ECO-SYSTEMS

All species rely on other insects, plants or birds in order to survive. This kind of relationship is called an eco-system. For example, many flowers produce nectar to lure honey-bees. The bees travel from flower to flower carrying pollen, a procedure necessary to fertilize these flowers. Many different types of plants and animals may be dependent on each other in this way in any eco-system.

SURVIVAL

As populations rise, and the existing countryside is put under greater pressure, more natural habitats are destroyed. Many plant and animal species are lost in this way – and it is a great loss. Different species are valuable in that they provide variety and should be saved for their own sake, but we can also learn from them. Many plants and animals have special properties that could be studied for human use, so it is important to preserve them.

Pandas, like many large animal species, are in danger of extinction. Smaller species, including bugs and plants, are also important but are disappearing without being noticed.

'We need to better protect and manage eco-systems for a safer more prosperous future.'

AGENDA 21

21

CASE STUDY

THE GREAT RAINFORESTS
OF THE WORLD

VALUABLE PROPERTIES

Many drugs used in medicine today originate from herbal medicine. Aspirin comes from willow bark; codeine and morphine come from poppies. Quinine is another plant extract used in drugs all over the world to combat malaria, a disease which is spread by the bite of the tropical mosquito. Many Europeans visiting Africa were killed by malaria before a drug was discovered by a combination of luck, accident and observation. It was found that the juice from the bark of a Peruvian cinchona tree both prevented and treated malaria; the juice contained quinine.

Quinine is extracted from the dried bark or trunk of the cinchona tree.

AGENDA 21 aims to:

- promote the wise use of resources
- prevent the waste of fuel
- cut air pollution to protect health
- stop acid rain

VALUABLE RESOURCES

Oil, coal and gas are found deep within the earth in many parts of the world. Now, the industries which find, dig up and distribute these fuels create the world's biggest businesses.

Oil, mined from platforms like this one off Norway, is used for fuel and to make plastics, nylon and other everyday items.

FUEL AND FUMES

Oil can be burnt like coal but can also be refined to make petrol and diesel. One of coal's main uses is in power stations where it is burnt to make electricity. All these processes produce smoke and cause pollution.

The chemical sulphur, contained in smoke, mixes with water in the atmosphere to create sulphuric acid. This falls as acid rain and damages the environment. All European and North American countries are now combating acid rain by taking the sulphur out of the smoke from power stations.

As the acid level of rivers and lakes rises, plant and animal life dies.

A CLEANER FUEL

Gas is tapped from the ground and distributed in pipelines to be used for central heating, cooking and powering factories. It is a much cleaner fuel than either coal or oil because it does not contain sulphur and other chemicals. However, just like all fossil fuels, it still produces a lot of carbon dioxide which contributes to the problem of global warming.

Gas escapes from underground as oil is collected. Rather than use the gas, a valuable resource in itself, it is wasted by being burnt.

CASE STUDY

GERMANY AND INDIA

IMPROVING TECHNOLOGY, REDUCING POLLUTION

Siemans Power Generation Group of Germany formed an agreement with Gharat Heavy Electricals Ltd of India to export the technology for highly efficient coal and gas driven turbines for producing electricity. The deal provided Germany with important export orders. It also provided India with technology to produce more electricity using less fuel and creating fewer harmful emissions. Both countries and both companies have gained.

Delhi, India, is a very polluted city, like many of the capitals around the world. This pollution could be reduced by using new technology.

WILL THEY RUN OUT?

Peat, oil, coal and gas are all non-renewable fuels – eventually they will run out. Before that happens the pollution caused by burning all these fuels will make life very unpleasant and cause environmental damage to the earth. World leaders have decided that it is important to cut down on burning these fuels as much as possible.

'Those who cause or threaten environmental harm should bear the full costs of controlling emissions and repairing the damage done by them.'

AGENDA 21

Agenda 21 encourages governments to make companies pay for cleaning up the pollution they cause.

'Transport is the fastest growing user of energy posing major problems of traffic jams, noise, health, _and_ countryside is disappearing under new roads.'

UK Electricity Association.

Cars, lorries and buses eat up fossil fuels. Alternative forms of transport need to be researched.

There are many ways to reduce the use of fossil fuels; cars could be produced to travel further on less fuel, people's homes could be better insulated so they need less gas, oil or coal to heat them. Light bulbs are being made that use one-fifth of the electricity used by standard bulbs, but produce the same brightness. It is hoped that through improvements in technology, alternative methods of fuelling industry can also be found.

Solar power, the renewable energy of the future, is put to industrial use in Spain at this solar power station.

CASE STUDY

EUROPE

CLEANER, CHEAPER TRANSPORT

Electric vehicles are on trial in several countries in Europe. At La Rochelle, France, parking places at homes and in the city centre have been provided with electricity points so people can plug in and recharge the batteries in their cars while they sleep or shop. In Köln, Germany, a similar system is being tested, but here the car batteries are powered by solar energy.

The running cost of electric cars is one-third of the price of petrol-driven cars and half the cost of cars run on diesel.

Not only is this car in Köln run on batteries, but the batteries are powered by the sun. This saves on money as well as resources.

- promote different forms of energy that do not cause pollution
- increase the knowledge and use of clean technology throughout the world
- promote recycling of existing resources

Recycling saves energy and resources.

ALTERNATIVE ENERGIES

WHAT IS RENEWABLE?

Coal, oil and gas can only be burned once and then are gone forever. But the wind blows most of the year, the sun comes up every morning and rivers flow continuously when they are fed by new rains. If these natural forces can be used to make electricity on a large scale, then energy can be constantly renewable.

'Industrial countries need to consume less resources, particularly energy, and reduce emissions. This means developing renewable energy.'

AGENDA 21

The technology now exists for windmills to drive turbines. It has long been possible to make electricity from water power, with river currents pushing wheels. Electricity can now be produced directly from sunlight and solar energy can also be used to heat water.

Wind farms, where wind is used to make electricity, are becoming big business in many countries.

ANOTHER ALTERNATIVE

Nuclear power was once seen as the great hope for the future. In the 1960s, the idea of producing unlimited power from tiny atoms crashing into each other captured the imagination of the world.

Since then, nuclear power has proved very expensive because it is dangerous and has to be carefully controlled. Getting rid of nuclear waste is another extremely serious problem. The waste remains damaging to human health and harms animal and plant life for thousands of years. As a result, developing nuclear power goes against many of the aims of Agenda 21 because the unsolved problems of this generation are passed on to the next.

A German worker lowers radioactive fuel rods into a special container for transporting the nuclear waste.

The oil industry, including companies like the China Petroleum Refinery in Taiwan, is one of the world's biggest employers.

COMPARING COSTS

Industries involved with the processing of oil, coal and gas employ thousands of people. Governments are reluctant to close factories and mines, putting many people out of work. Additionally, relying on coal, oil and gas has previously seemed cheaper than taking on the costs of developing new technologies. However, if the cost of the pollution created by burning fossil fuels is taken into account, clean, renewable technologies are more attractive.

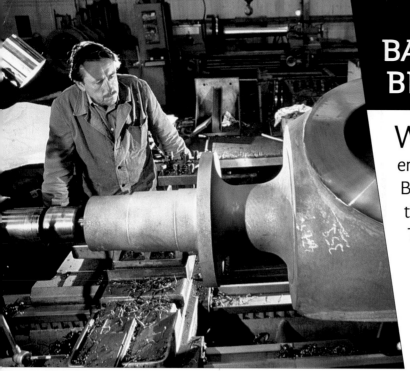

BACK TO THE BEGINNING

Wind, sun, wave and tidal power are energies of the past and of the future. Building new wind farms is now cheaper than building coal-fired power stations. The price of electricity generated by the sun through solar panels is still very high but is falling as more of the special solar panels are made. Producing such panels will soon be big business too.

By increasing the production and use of wind turbines, making electricity from wind will become cheaper than making it from coal.

'Renewable energy sources were for millions of years the only sources of energy for life on earth. This will happen again in the near future.'

Hermann Scheer,
President of Eurosolar, 1997.

CASE STUDY

SWITZERLAND

SOLAR POWER

Global warming is a very real threat. In Switzerland it is causing glaciers to melt and less snow to fall in the winter. This affects the country's tourist trade, as the skiing season is cut short. In turn, this affects Switzerland's wealth. The government decided to promote the use of solar energy in order to cut carbon dioxide emissions and reduce global warming. Already 43 school projects to install solar panels are underway. Many schools are producing more electricity than they need.

By selling the 'free' surplus electricity, the Swiss schools are not only providing a non-polluting energy source, but are also making a profit.

RENEWABLE AND REUSABLE

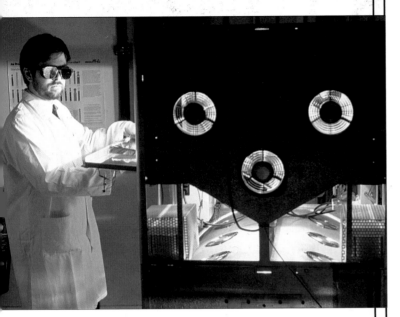

British scientists experiment to perfect photo-voltaic cells so they can produce electricity as cheaply as possible.

Solar power is considered to be the future source for providing electricity. Photo-voltaic cells, used to collect the sun's energy, have the advantage that they can be set up anywhere and produce electricity instantly without any pollution. This is valuable for people in poor countries with no electricity at all at present.

'Renewable energy currently provides 2% of the world's supplies. A vast expansion is needed to meet energy needs in the next century.'

World Energy Council report, 1996.

Scientists today are working on wave and tidal power. The technology works, but is still expensive. Together, renewable sources of energy could provide enough power for the whole world and bring pollution down to a fraction of the current level.

People can help save our world's resources by using renewable sources of energy as they become available. The more people who use them, the cheaper they will become. By combining renewable energies with the careful recycling of existing materials, we will move closer to becoming a sustainable society.

As renewable energy sources, such as tidal power, become more widely available they will also become less expensive.

GLOSSARY

atoms: tiny particles that make up all matter. Splitting atoms releases huge power and heat.

ban: when an activity is not allowed by law or official rules.

bio-diversity: the variety of plant and animal life.

cultivate: to prepare soil in order to grow food crops.

dam: a barrier built across a river to hold back the water.

deforestation: cutting down or destroying trees to use the wood or turn the forests into farm land.

developed country: a country that relies on money from industry and in which factories provide more jobs than agriculture.

developing country: a country that relies on agriculture, rather than on manufacturing goods for export, for example.

eco-system: the network of animals and plants which interact with and depend on each other in a locality.

emissions: smoke, gases, liquids or other substances left over after industrial processing, for example, the smoke caused by burning coal to make electricity.

energy: the power that is needed to create activity or movement. For example, fossil fuels are burned to create heat which can be used to power an engine.

evaporates: when a solid or liquid is turned into a gas, for example, when water is heated it evaporates into steam.

fertile: productive or fruitful. Fertile soil is rich in goodness and so produces excellent crops.

irrigate: to artificially water crops.

non-renewable: something that cannot be replaced. Once a non-renewable resource, such as oil, is taken from the environment it is gone permanently.

ozone layer: ozone is a special gas, including oxygen, that is in the atmosphere. A layer of the gas about 20 km to 25 km above the earth's surface acts as a barrier to harmful rays from the sun.

renewable: something that can be replaced or regrown, for example trees; or a source of energy that never runs out, such as the sun or wind.

reservoir: an artificial or natural lake that stores water.

resources: a stock or supply of a material.

sanitation: the provision of toilets and washing facilities to help people to keep clean and to dispose of sewage.

species: the dividing of different birds and animals into family groups.

sustainable: in this instance, to be able to maintain lifestyles or preserve resources over a long period of time.

turbines: a motor or machine driven by water, steam or gas to create energy or electricity.

virus: tiny disease-producing agents that cause colds and other illnesses.

FURTHER INFORMATION

Centre for Alternative Technology
Machynlleth
Powys, Wales,
SY0 9AZ UK
Tel: 01654 702400
info@catinfo.demon.co.uk
www.foe.co.uk/CAT

WaterAid
Prince Consort House
27-29 Albert Embankment
London, SE1 7UB, UK
Tel: 0171 793 4500

United Nations Association
Sustainable Development Unit
3 Whitehall Court
London, SW1A 2EL, UK
Tel: 0171 839 1784

World Wide Fund for Nature
Panda House
Weyside Park
Godalming
Surrey, GU7 1XR, UK
Tel: 01483 426444

Energy Australia
Tel: 13 15 25

Energy Resource of Australia
1 Macquarie Place
Sydney 2000
AUSTRALIA
Tel: 02 9256 8900

Department of Energy
29 Christie Street
St. Leonards
NSW 2065
AUSTRALIA
Tel: 02 9901 8888

Land and Water Conservation
23-33 Bridge Street
Sydney 2000
AUSTRALIA
Toll Free: 1800 641 596

INDEX